COPYRIGH LAW vs. FILE SHARING IN EUROPE

COPYRIGHT HOLDERS vs. INTERNET INTERMEDIARIES AND USERS

TODOR A. SHUKEROV

Todor A. Shukerov holds a LLM International Commercial Law degree from University of Nottingham and a Master of Law degree from University of Plovdiv.

After his graduation from University of Plovdiv Todor completed a traineeship programme at Bulgarian courts. Subsequently, Todor was awarded with an EU Taught Masters Scholarship from University of Nottingham where he was accepted in the LLM International Commercial Law course.

During his studies in University of Nottingham Todor specialised in Intellectual Property Law, EU Competition Law and International Sale of Goods. In his dissertation, entitled *"COPYRIGH LAW vs. FILE SHARING IN EUROPE"* and awarded with Distinction, Todor analysed the legal framework in relation to peer-to-peer file sharing technology in Europe. This dissertation was used as a basis of this book. The book was completed in Nottingham, in March 2010.

After the completion of his studies in University of Nottingham Todor provided legal, administrative and commercial support to German investors developing a 12-MW photovoltaic (solar) power plant in Bulgaria, a project amounted to nearly EUR 25 millions and successfully finished in the summer of 2012.

In his professional experience in the Council of the EU (at the Industry, Space, Research and Innovation Unit of Directorate General Economic Affairs and Competitiveness) and in the course of negotiations concerning the research and training of the European Atomic Energy Community (2014 - 2018), part of Horizon 2020 programme, Todor carried out in-depth research and analysis of the European Union nuclear energy policy which resulted in a book entitled *"EU NUCLEAR ENERGY POLICY"*.

The author alone is responsible for the facts and opinions expressed in this book.

2013

Brussels

COPYRIGH LAW vs. FILE SHARING IN EUROPE

COPYRIGHT HOLDERS vs. INTERNET INTERMEDIARIES AND USERS

CONTENTS

1. INTRODUCTION

The global spread of Internet and digital technologies have led to clash between the rights of copyright holders and interests of users. The global network and modern technologies significantly facilitate the communication and dissemination of information in the on-line environment. This feature renders the distribution of existing copyright works at very low cost, in many cases even free of charge, which lead to disturbance in the beneficial effect of intellectual property protection. For example, if a single digital copy is made available and distributed on Internet, especially via peer-to-peer (P2P) file sharing networks, this leads to thousands, even millions of identical, unauthorised copies that harm the copyright holders' creative activity and investment.[1] As a result, the traditional incentive/reward rationale for copyright protection is seriously undermined. Therefore, it is not surprising that over the last decade right holders have initiated massive battle against Internet users which comprised several fronts. Firstly, legal enforcement actions have been brought not only to users, but also to P2P network distributors and internet service providers (ISPs). Secondly, due to political lobbying, new legislature have been introduced to combat and prevent infringing activities carried out through the use of file sharing services. Thirdly, technological protection measures have been introduced to either suspend illegal copying or circumvent such acts. And fourthly, in order the public to be persuaded of the detrimental impact of illegal file sharing on entertainment industry, especially on

---

[1] "In 2007 10 billion unauthorised music copies were shared via P2P networks worldwide and up to 80 percent of the Internet traffic was consisted of copyright infringing files". IFPI Digital Music Report, January 2008 (http://www.ifpi.org/content/library/dmr2008.pdf).

struggling artists, huge educational campaign has been organised.

In contrast, the fundamental feature of Internet is the freedom to communicate and exchange information. Internet users, P2P software providers and ISPs have argued that restrictions of file sharing services could restrain unduly other lawful Internet activities. Accordingly, some on-line antipiracy legislature and acts, such as tracing users' private accounts, could limit unjustifiably "the exercise by any person of one's right to express oneself and freely communicate".[2] Furthermore, it was noted that the broad obligations imposed to ISPs to monitor their networks and to disclose the personal data of their subscribers render them to act as public authorities such as general censor or security, defence and police forces.

However, it is worth pointing out that not all file sharing services are illegal. The spread of P2P technology on Internet has promoted new ways of commercial distribution, such as paid on-line stores and file sharing websites, which have increased the sale of audio-visual works and have benefited copyright holders.[3] P2P networks have also enabled new authors and artists to distribute some of their works for advertising and promotions purposes. Whereas it is common practice a first single (album) or episode of new musician or series respectively, to be distributed

---

[2] French Constitutional Council (Court), 10 June 2009. The Court rejected three-strike draft law proposed on the grounds that it was infringing the Constitution and the Declaration of the Rights of Man and of the Citizen from.
[3] "Music companies' digital revenues internationally grew by an estimated 25per cent in 2008 to US 3.7 billion" IFPI Digital Music Report, January 2009 (http://www.ifpi.org/content/section_resources/dmr2009.html).

free of charge via file sharing systems, it can be seen that even well-known artists have offered their repertoire for free download[4] or for "pay as much as you want".[5]

In the new digital world comprising P2P technology and other information location tools, the copyright in Europe has been confronted with real and difficult challenge, namely to fit appropriately its long standing copyright principles and rules and thus, to find justifiable balance between the rights of copyright holders and the interests of others. The aim of present analysis is to evaluate critically the application of copyright law to infringing activities performed by use of file sharing services. In next chapter various P2P networks and participants engaged in such infringing activates will be illustrated together with the relevant International and European legislature. Some national courts' decisions in respect to primary infringement will be also discussed. However, copyright law has never limited liability only to the person who personally commits the act of infringement. Such liability generally is extended to those who encourage, assist or benefits from someone else's infringing act. Accordingly in the third chapter, different approaches to secondary liability and their application by European national courts in the field of on-line copyright infringement will be reviewed as initially, references will be made to the United States and Australian doctrines and case law. The fourth chapter will offer comprehensive analysis of European developments on secondary liability rules that determine the role and liability of ISPs.

---

[4] For example, in January 2006 *Arctic Monkeys* have made available for free download their early recordings.
[5] In October 2007 *Radiohead* released the album *In Rainbows* via digital download only, with fans being able to decide how much to pay for the album.

Furthermore, it can be noted that a number of potential solutions have been proposed so far, but only two of them provide more balanced copyright system in relation to P2P networks. Therefore, the fifth chapter will focus only on watermarking and encryption as part of technological protection measures, and on the private copyright levy.

2. FILE SHARING AND PRIMARY COPYRIGH INFRINGEMENT

2.1 Peer-to-peer file sharing

P2P file sharing process takes place on Internet, which is a global telecommunications system of interconnected public, private, governmental, local, academic and business networks that are accessible via the use of computers. Internet operates on the basis of standard protocols, such as Internet protocol (IP) and hypertext transfer protocol (HTTP), and packet switching technology. Currently over 1.6 billion people use Internet worldwide.[6] In general, there are three participants who are engaged directly or indirectly in on-line illegal exchange of copyright material. Internet users or end users are persons who perform primary acts of infringements. By uploading and downloading files consisting audio-visual protected works, they make acts of reproduction, distribution, communication or adaptation which are in violation of copyright holders' rights. Internet intermediary is a term which refers to a person or a legal person who is not directly involved in unlawful acts, but who is somehow connected with the file sharing. There are several activity-related words regularly used for such participant, namely third party, service provider, contributor, inciter or accomplice. In the present analysis the terms third party, software provider or distributor will be used to identify the intermediaries, which by developing, providing, maintaining and monitoring P2P software and websites, facilitate file sharing infringing activities. The EU E-

---

[6] According to Internet World Statistics from 30 June 2009, 1 668 870 408 30 people use Internet. (http://www.Internetworlsstats.com/stats.htm).

Commerce Directive[7] interpreted broadly the concept of service provider comprising all providers of information society services, whether Internet-based or otherwise.[8] However, for the sake of clarity the term service provider or Internet service provider (ISP) will be applied to telecommunications companies that supply and maintain an Internet connectivity and access between two or more users and that host P2P networks.

File sharing is making available of files for transfer and copying from user's computer to other users over the Internet and respectively, the receiving of files made available in this way.[9] Therefore, this process takes place between networks of users and includes the acts of uploading and downloading. P2P software administrators provide technologies and services required to connect users and enable them to perform such transfer within the particular file sharing network. The first generation P2P networks, such as *Napster*, allowed users to connect to a central server in order to upload a list of files to be transmitted and to search for the location of files on other users. Then, the server provides the information required for users enabling them to start a direct exchange of files between their computers (nodes). In contrast, the second generation of P2P networks, such as *Kazaa*, are decentralised. Users, by connecting to one or more computers with high bandwidth and processing

[7] Directive 2000/31/EC of the European Parliament and of the Council of 8 June 2000 on certain legal aspects of information society services, in particular electronic commerce, in the Internal Market [2000] OJ L178/1.
[8] Ibid., Art.2 (a)-(b).
[9] A. N. Dixon, "Liability of users and third parties for copyright infringements on the internet: overview of international developments" (*Peer-to-peer file sharing and secondary liability in copyright law* edited by A. Strowel, Edward Elgar 2009), at page 14.

power (supernodes), are able to transfer and exchange index information. Subsequently, the supernodes communicate between themselves in order to locate the data requested and reply to users' computers. As a result, the file sharing takes place directly between the users.

Similarly to the previous generation file sharing systems, third generation P2P networks, such as *BitTorent*, enable simultaneous downloading and uploading of protected files. However, unlike second generation P2P networks, the *BitTorent* software renders the transfer of files much quickly and efficiently due to use of advanced technology called swarming, which allows users to obtain pieces of a file from different computers simultaneously based on a packet data transmission.[10] Furthermore, such third generation P2P networks are designed with built-in encryption and anonymity features, which hinder the tracing of users' computers (nodes) and data exchanged.

2.2 International and European legislature related to file sharing

The development of new technologies, such as Internet, posed the question whether and how copyright protection could be fitted within, whether copyright should be applied to electronically (even sometimes temporally) stored, transmitted and used copies and how the long standing copyright concepts of reproduction and distribution, typically covered articles in

---

[10] O. B. Vincents, "When rights clash online: the tracking of P2P copyright infringements vs. the EC Personal Data Directive" [2008] IJL & IT 16(3), 270-296.

tangible form, could be applied to on-line storage, transmission and use. In middle 1990s, international community decided that copyright should cover not only the storage in digital form and on-line transmission, but also the act of making available of copyright material for access on Internet and thus on-line users' activities became regulated.[11] Copyright protection granted to authors, performers and producers of phonograms was implemented in Europe by the EU Information Society Directive[12], which extended the exclusive rights given from WIPO Treaties to film producers and broadcasting organisations.[13]

---

[11] WIPO Copyright Treaty (WCT), Art. 8: "Without prejudice to the provisions of the Berne Convention, authors of literary and artistic works shall enjoy the exclusive right of authorizing any communication to the public of their works, by wire or wireless means, including the making available to the public of their works in such a way that members of the public may access these works from a place and at a time individually chosen by them".
WIPO Performances and Phonograms Treaty (WPPT), Art. 10: "Performers shall enjoy the exclusive right of authorizing the making available to the public of their performances fixed in phonograms, by wire or wireless means, in such a way that members of the public may access them from a place and at a time individually chosen by them" and Art. 14: "Producers of phonograms shall enjoy the exclusive right of authorizing the making available to the public of their phonograms, by wire or wireless means, in such a way that members of the public may access them from a place and at a time individually chosen by them". (Both adopted in Geneva on December 20, 1996).
[12] Directive 2001/29/EC of the European Parliament and of the Council of 22 May 2001 on the harmonisation of certain aspects of copyright and related rights in the information society [2001] OJ L167/10.
[13] Ibid., Art. 3: "(1) Member States shall provide authors with the exclusive right to authorise or prohibit any communication to the public of their works, by wire or wireless means, including the making available to the public of their works in such a way that members of the public may access them from a place and at a time individually chosen by them.
(2) Member States shall provide for the exclusive right to authorise or prohibit the making available to the public, by wire or wireless means, in such a way that members of the public may access them from a place and at a time individually chosen by them:
(a) for performers, of fixations of their performances;
(b) for phonogram producers, of their phonograms;
(c) for the producers of the first fixations of films, of the original and copies of their films;
(d) for broadcasting organisations, of fixations of their broadcasts, whether these broadcasts are transmitted by wire or over the air, including by cable or satellite.
(3) The rights referred to in paragraphs 1 and 2 shall not be exhausted by any act of communication to the public or making available to the public as set out in this

However, the scope of copyright holders' exclusive right was reduced by the Agreed Statement to WIPO Copyright Treaty which stated that the mere provision of physical facilities for enabling or making a communication does not in itself amount to communication.[14] In order to harmonise the different approaches taken by Member States towards service providers, EU E-Commerce Directive adopted similar legislative provisions. By introducing liability exemptions for those who essentially play a passive role in transmitting and storing information, the Directive intended to eliminate any legal obstacles that may hamper the exercise of freedom of establishment and freedom to provide services.[15] Accordingly, nowadays service providers are exempted from civil and criminal liability for all types of infringing acts performed by third parties even though they may be subject to preliminary injunctions, when certain requirements are met.[16]

The enforcement of intellectual property rights was implemented by EU Enforcement Directive,[17] which object was to approximate national legislative systems so as to ensure high and homogenous application of civil remedies by domestic courts.[18]

Article".
[14] Agreed Statements Concerning Article 8, WIPO Copyright Treaty adopted in Geneva on 20 December 1996:"It is understood that the mere provision of physical facilities for enabling or making a communication does not in itself amount to communication within the meaning of this Treaty or the Berne Convention. It is further understood that nothing in Article 8 precludes a Contracting Party from applying limitations, in form of statutory or compulsory licences, in connection to broadcasting and related rights by them".
[15] Directive 2000/31/EC, recitals 5 and 6.
[16] The exemptions from service providers' liability will be discussed in the third chapter below.
[17] Directive 2004/48/EC of the European Parliament and of the Council of 29 April 2004 on the enforcement of intellectual property rights [2004] OJ L195/16.
[18] Ibid., recital 10.

The Directive harmonises the civil rules on standing, evidence, interlocutory measures, seizure, injunctions, damages, costs and judicial publication, but does not cover any criminal offences. It can be noted that the Directive regulates only the enforcement of intellectual property rights, but not the rights themselves. Furthermore, the European Commission has proposed a criminal enforcement Directive for intellectual property rights, including standard accomplice's liability provision.[19] According to the recommendation from the European Parliament, the provision "shall ensure that all international infringements of intellectual property rights on a commercial scale, and aiding or abetting and inciting the actual infringement, are treated as criminal offences".[20] However, the proposed draft of the Directive is still under consideration.

2.3 Primary liability of Internet users

On-line transmission and use of copyright material via P2P networks without authorisation of relevant copyright holders may raise two grounds on which a party can be sued for an infringement - primary (direct) and secondary (indirect). A direct infringement takes place when a user performs acts, such as copying and posting (uploading) work on Internet, within the range of someone else's exclusive right without his permission or consent. Generally, an indirect infringement occurs where a

---

[19] Amended proposal for a Directive of the European Parliament and of the Council on criminal measures aimed at ensuring the enforcement of intellectual property rights Brussels, 26 April 2006 COM(2006) 168 final 2005/0127 (COD).
[20] . European Parliament legislative resolution of 25 April 2007 on the amended proposal for a directive of the European Parliament and of the Council on criminal measures aimed at ensuring the enforcement of intellectual property rights (COM(2006)0168 - C6-0233/2005 - 2005/0127(COD)) [2008] *OJ C 74E/526.*

person intentionally or negligently facilitate, contribute or participate in someone else's direct infringing act by assisting, encouraging or sanctioning such primary illegal activity or use material derived from it.[21] As it will be seen in next chapter the imposition of secondary liability requires presence of actual knowledge or knowledge that the indirect infringer is presumed to have due to his business activity, as well as some other elements.

National courts in Europe had opportunity to explore the imposition of primary liability on sharing copyright content over P2P networks in many cases. For example, in Germany a user was held liable for "offering of recordings for downloading which violates reproduction and/or making available rights",[22] as well as a P2P website operator for making available of infringing music files from his own server.[23] An Internet account holder was also found liable for making "his Internet connection available to his underage son" because of "his duty to stop illegal conduct".[24] Similarly, in United Kingdom the Court concluded as a direct infringement, the act of connecting computer to Internet which was running P2P software where the files were placed in shared directory and it was irrelevant whether the account holder was aware of other's infringing actions.[25] In August 2009, a file sharer was ordered to pay GBP 16 000 to a video game publisher for illicit transfer of a computer game via P2P network on Internet.[26]

---

[21] P. Akester, *A practical guide to digital copyright law*, Sweet & Maxwell (2008), at page 37.
[22] Case No 28 O 634/05 Koln District Court, 2005.
[23] *Monrex Rolex v. Ricardo* No I ZR 304/01 German Civil Supreme Court, 2004.
[24] Case No 308 O 41/06 Hamburg District Court, 2006.
[25] *Polydor v. Brown* [2005] EWHC 3191.
[26] *Topware Interactive v. Barwinska* Decision of Patents County Court, August

In 2005, as a result of the modification of the Italian copyright law courts could impose administrative penalties for users who download and penal sanctions for those who upload and share copyright material with other subscribers. Subsequently, in January 2006 the Italian operator of the file sharing website *OpenNap*, as an alternative to two months imprisonment, was fined for having shared music files to about 2 500 users.

In contrast, some national courts have rejected to apply primary liability on the basis of the private copyright exception. For instance, a French court found an individual who was shared files via P2P network not liable for primary copyright infringement on the grounds that the copyright material exchanged was used for personal rather than commercial purposes.[27] Likewise, in Spain the Criminal Court of Santander dismissed a case against an Internet user on the basis that the files shared were for private use.[28]

Although the users as primary infringers could be chased easier, the initiation of legal proceedings against them is connected with curtain difficulties. Firstly, the enormous number of users sharing protected material through P2P networks amounts to thousands, sometimes even to millions, and thus it is not economically feasible all of them to be sued. Secondly, in order for legal actions to be brought against direct infringers, the right holders

---

2009, M. Starmer, "Video game company hunts down individual gamers in clampdown on illicit peer to peer file sharing" [2009] Ent. L.R. 20(1), 28-29.
[27] *Société Civile des Producteurs Phonographiques v. Anthony G* 31 chambre/2 (8 December 2005).
[28] E. Batalla, "Spain: Decision on file sharing for private use" Batalla Abodagos, Madrid, July 2006.

must obtain discovery of identity orders directed to ISPs, which are subject to separate legal proceedings before the Court. Whereas the pursuit of file sharers is expensive, time-consuming and legally complex, it is economically and virtually efficient for copyright holders to target facilitators of the file sharing, namely P2P software providers and distributors.

3. SECONDARY LIABILITY OF FILE SHARING SERVICE PROVIDERS

3.1 US and Australian approaches and case law to secondary liability

Generally, the law in the area of indirect infringement by Internet P2P file sharing service providers derives from common law and civil law legal principles and rules. Each legal system provides statutory and case law specifically related to the copyright characterised with different approaches to a third party liability in the field of on-line copyright infringement. The very first case against a P2P network provider was initiated on the other side of the Atlantic whereas the Australian authorisation theory is similar to European civil law doctrines of secondary copyright liability. Therefore, it is worth mentioning the key principles and decisions in USA and Australia related to P2P file sharing.

In the US law two approaches towards an indirect copyright infringement have been applied traditionally, namely contributory liability and vicarious liability. A contributory liability is applied in cases where a third party knows or suspects a direct infringement and contributes materially to the act of infringement of another.[29] However, in *Sony Beatamax*[30] case it was held that the intent to cause infringement could not be imposed solely on the manufacture and on the sale of recording equipment capable of substantial legitimate non-infringing use for which the

---

[29] *Gershwin Publishing v. Columbia Artist Management* 1162 (2d Cir. 1971): "...where a third party with knowledge of the infringing activity induces couses or materially contributes to the infringing act of another."
[30] *Sony Corp. v. Universal City Studios* 464 US 417 (1984).

manufacturer knew was used in some cases for copyright infringement. A vicarious liability arises where an indirect infringer has the right and ability to monitors or controls the actions of primary infringement performed by others and receives financial benefits from the infringing conduct.[31]

In July 1999, alleging a copyright infringement, members of music industry initiated legal proceedings against *Napster*, an Internet company that maintained a central server, which was facilitating the transfer of music files between its clients through indexing and searching of MP3 files. In order to upload a list of files or search for the location of other users' files, the *Napster* clients had to connect to the central server where they received the necessary information for a direct user-to-user P2P transmission of MP3 files. Both doctrines of indirect copyright infringement were applied and the Court concluded that *Napster* had materially contributed to the primary infringing acts by means of encouraging and assisting its clients to infringe record companies' copyright rights.[32] As to the vicarious copyright infringement it was found that *Napster* gained financial benefits from the failure to supervise its own website and thus a vicarious liability was imposed.[33]

---

[31] *Shapiro, Bernstein & Co v. H.L. Green* 306 (2d Cir. 1963).

[32] *A & M v. Napster* 114 F. Supp.2d 896 (N.D. Call. 2000): "One who, with knowledge of infringing activity, induces, causes or materially contributes to the infringing conduct by another, may be held liable as a contributory infringer".

[33] Ibid.,: " In the context of copyright law, vicarious liability extends beyond an employer/employee relationship to cases in which defendant has the right and ability to supervise the infringing activity and also has direct financial interest in such activates".

The file sharing software offered and maintained by *Napster* was first generation P2P network operated with a central server. In contrast, the second and third generations file sharing networks do not contain a central server managing list of files. Unlike *Napster*, they are decentralised hybrid systems and their primary goal is to transfer information directly between users. The involvement of file sharing system developers and distributors is limited to provision of software enabling their clients to establish connections with other computers using the same network software. Such P2P network was subject to the proceeding in *MGM Studio v. Grokster*[34] where the Court expanded the secondary liability by finding *Grokster*'s owners, who distributed a network with an object to promote its use for copyright infringement or other affirmative steps to foster infringement, liable for users' infringing acts. The Court built its judgment on the inducement liability, which derives from the US patent law[35] and imposes secondary liability for those who induce others to infringe the copyright. *Sony Batemax* case was distinguished on the basis that a mere design of a product which is capable of substantial non-infringing uses does not preclude secondary liability where there is a clear intention to induce.[36] However, the Court failed to define what amounts to substantial non–infringing use and thus in future cases a file sharing service provider may

---

[34] 125 S. Ct. 2764 (2005).
[35] USC, Ch.35, s. 271(b)"...whoever actively induces infringement of a patent shall be liable as an infringer."
[36] The evidence of intent found by the Court included the Grokster' attempts to attract the former Napster's users, the unavailability of filtering mechanism which would reduce the amount of copyright infringement committed by Grokster' clients and the fact that the increase of software use led to the increase of the advertising-related profits too.

be covered by the *Sony Batemax* defence, but at the same time to be found liable under the inducement theory.[37]

In Australia, as well as in other Commonwealth countries, a secondary liability for copyright infringement originates from the notion of authorisation. Under the common law there is a long-standing principle that it is unlawful to authorise another person to infringe copyright, as the word authorise does not only mean a mere grant of licence for use of copyright material, but it is also understood as "sanction, approve and countenance".[38] In addition, the notion of authorisation covers such third party activities as "permit" or even "treat with inactivity or indifference".[39] In *Moorhouse*[40] case, it was held that a university library that offered a coin-operated photocopy service had implemented inadequate monitoring and warnings against the users of photocopiers and thus was liable for authorising copyright infringement. In 2000, the developments of the offence of authorisation in Australian case law were adopted in the Australian Copyright Act 1968 by means of three part test of authorisation which requires three factors to be considered in defining authorisation, namely control, relationship and due care.[41]

---

[37] P. Akester, *A practical guide to digital copyright law*, Sweet & Maxwell (2008), at page 53; Also in the ongoing case *Arista Records v. Lime Wire* (NY District Court No 06 CV 5936 GEL) the Court continues to explore the third party copyright liability on the basis of *Gokster* decision.

[38] *Falcon v. Famous Players Film* [1926] 2 KB 474. The definition of authorisation in question has been adopted in most subsequent courts in the UK and Australia.

[39] *Adelaide Corp. v. Australasian Performing Right Association* [1928] 40 CLR 481.

[40] *University of New South Wales v. Moorhouse* [1975] 133 CLR 1.

[41] Australian Copyright Act 1968, s.36 (1A):" In determining ... whether or not a person has authorised the doing in Australia of any act comprised in the copyright in a work, without the licence of the owner of the copyright, the matters that must be taken into account include the following:

(a) the extent (if any) of the person's power to prevent the doing of the act concerned;

(b) the nature of any relationship existing between the person and the person

In 2005, a secondary liability based on the authorisation theory was applied in a case which involved P2P network software. In *Universal Music Australia v. Sharman Licence Holding*[42] the Australian Federal Court, rejecting *Sherman*'s defence under Section 112e of the Australian Copyright Act,[43] found six individuals and companies related to *Kazaa* file sharing service liable for authorising users' copyright infringing acts, on the basis of the following findings: supply and maintenance of facilities intended for infringement; *Kazaa* P2P network was used for sharing of copyright infringing files predominantly; defendants had long known that their system was used for copyright infringement and even they had encouraged its use through a marketing campaign; *Kazaa* software providers had financial interest in maximising infringement; and they failed to prevent users' infringement by means of filtering tools and adequate warnings. In addition, the Court ordered defendants to pay 90 per cent of plaintiff's costs and to come back for damages hearings. However, in 2006 the parties settled the litigation as *Kazaa* related defendants agreed to pay USD 100 million and to implement filtering technology for preventing future illegal file sharing.[44]

---

who did the act concerned;
(c) whether the person took any reasonable steps to prevent or avoid the doing of the act, including whether the person complied with any relevant industry codes of practice".
[42] [2005] FCA 1242.
[43] Australian Copyright Act 1968, s.112e:" A person (including a carrier or carriage service provider) who provides facilities for making, or facilitating the making of, a communication is not taken to have authorised any infringement of copyright in an audio-visual item merely because another person uses the facilities so provided to do something the right to do which is included in the copyright".
[44] "Kazaa settles with record industry and goes legitimate" IFPI Resources 27 July 2006 (http.ifpi.org/content/section_resources/piracy-report-current.html).

3.2 European approaches to secondary liability

Similarly to Australia, United Kingdom implemented the authorisation theory under both the statutory[45] and case law.[46] However, it should be noted that in some cases within English law, authorising another person to perform act restricted by copyright, without right holder's permission, could be qualified as an act of primary infringement itself.[47] A secondary liability for unauthorised copying was found in *Sony Music v. Easyinternetcafe*[48] where the customers of defendants' Internet cafes were able to download various files on cafes' central server and copy thus stored files onto a CD afterwards. Neither cafes' staff, which was assisting the unauthorised copying, nor the coffee shop customers had any permission from the copyright holders concerned. In contrast, in *CBS Records v. Amstrad*[49] the House of Lords held that a mere production of an equipment enabling users to infringe someone else's copyright does not make a manufacturer liable for a secondary infringement unless he had specific knowledge of the actual infringement. In the particular situation a provider of double cassette duplication

---

[45] UK Copyright, Design and Patent Act 1988, s. 16(2):" Copyright in a work is infringed by a person who without the licence of the copyright owner does, or authorises another to do, any of the acts restricted by the copyright";
s. 16(3):" References in this Part to the doing of an act restricted by the copyright in a work are to the doing of it— (a) in relation to the work as a whole or any substantial part of it, and
(b) either directly or indirectly".
[46] For instance, purchasing agents, juke box providers, bandstand owners and other similar third parties were held liable for authorising the infringement of the others.
[47] P. Akester, *A practical guide to digital copyright law*, Sweet & Maxwell (2008), at page 37.
[48] [2003] EWHC 62.
[49] [1988] AC 1013.

equipment gave warnings that an authorisation was required for some copying which he was not entitled to give and the use of equipment after sale was out of his control. Hence the Court concluded that users had discretion to determine whether and what could be copied and there were no grounds for raise of secondary liability under the authorisation theory.

In addition, under English law the courts may find an indirect infringement based on the common law doctrines of joint tortfeasor liability and criminal law accomplice liability. Under the first approach a third party could be held liable if he/she is involved in a common design with someone who commits infringement in pursuance of that design.[50] In relation to the latter, in rare cases a secondary liability can be applied to a person who knowingly incites (encourages, threatens and endeavour to persuade), aids or procure another to commit a criminal copyright offence.[51]

In European civil law countries the acts of indirect infringement are assessed under provisions which cover the duty of care to avoid or not to cause damages to others and which may be applied to copyright law. Generally, the duty of care requires an obligation for acting reasonably to prevent harm to others and depends on the facts and circumstances in each particular case. Under the French law any act which causes damage to others

---

[50] *In The Koursk* [1924] All ER Rep 168, also approved in *CBS Records v. Amstrad* [1988] AC 1013.
[51] A. N. Dixon, "Liability of users and third parties for copyright infringements on the internet: overview of international developments" (*Peer-to-peer file sharing and secondary liability in copyright law* edited by A. Strowel, Edward Elgar 2009), at page 18.

obliges the person causing the damage to repair it.[52] Everyone is also responsible for damages causes by his acts or by his negligence.[53] Therefore, a secondary liability arises for inciting an accomplishment of infringing act on the basis of the civil reparation rule and criminal law nation of complicity. In Germany, if several persons perform unlawful act and cause damage jointly then each of those persons would be liable for such damage.[54] In application of this provision the German courts consider whether the defendant had induced or contributed to infringing act on the basis of a number of factors, namely the defendant's intention and knowledge of the infringing circumstances; the extent of defendant's duty to control his own activities; the required degree of such supervision; and the existence of reckless act by defendant leading to dangerous situation.[55] Frequently, in determining whether the duty of care has been violated the courts in Europe look at the economic benefit of the third party involved in the infringement and through cost-benefit analysis, including the cost of harm, the cost of avoidance and the magnitude of harm, they define the subsequent remedies.[56]

---

[52] French Civil Code, Art. 1382:" Any act whatever of man, which causes damage to another, obliges the one by whose fault it occurred, to compensate it".
[53] Ibid., Art. 1383:" Everyone is liable for the damage he causes not only by his intentional act, but also by his negligent conduct or by his imprudence".
[54] German Civil Code (BGB Bundesgesetzbuch), Art. 830:" (1) If more than one person has caused damage by a jointly committed tort, then each of them is responsible for the damage. The same applies if it cannot be established which of several persons involved caused the damage by his act; (2) Instigators and accessories are equivalent to joint tortfeasors".
[55] J.A.L Sterling, *World Copyright Law*, Sweet & Maxwell 3rd edition (2008), at page 629.
[56] K. Koelman & B. Hugenholtz, "Online service provider liability for copyright liability" WIPO Workshop (9-10 December 1999).

In the European jurisdictions, a third party's liability could be also imposed under either civil or criminal law where a person knowingly assists in infringing acts of others. For example, in *TONO v. Bruvik*[57] the Norwegian Supreme Court held defendants liable for users' illegal transfer of music files via hyperlinks on *Bruvik*'s website due to their deliberate assistance and undoubted awareness of such uploading and downloading without the consent of right holders.

As it has been seen, in order a defendant to be found guilty some actions of indirect infringement require his knowledge about the infringing nature of copyrights involved. Furthermore, in determining whether knowledge is necessary to constitute a certain infringement, a reference can only be made to the particular domestic law within the European Union. However, such enforcement issue in copyright law may be overcome by an injunctive relief against a third party. The EU Information Society Directive obliges the Members States to make prospective injunctions available to copyright holders against intermediaries whose services are used for copyright infringement although the intermediaries themselves may not be liable for the infringement.[58] Even before the introduction of the Directive, civil law principles allowed preliminary injunctions against third parties engaged in someone else's tort without prior knowledge of infringing actions. The doctrine of *Storerhaftung* in Germany enables an injunctive relief against third parties involved in positive acts that cause

---

[57] Case No 2004/822, Supreme Court, Norway (25 January 2005).
[58] Directive 2001/29/EC, Art. 8(3): " Member States shall ensure that rightholders are in a position to apply for an injunction against intermediaries whose services are used by a third party to infringe a copyright or related right ".

disturbance although damages would not be laid down without proof of knowledge.[59]

3.3 Application of European approaches to secondary liability by national courts

The current analysis will turn now to some key decision in relation to file sharing service providers' liability for infringing acts performed by users of their P2P software with an aim to illustrate how and to what extent the application of aforementioned approaches in Europe could hold indirect copyright infringement. In summary proceedings regarding a licence dispute between the file sharing network *Kazaa* and the Dutch authors collecting society *Buma/Stemra*, the latter counterclaimed that *Kazaa* software had infringed its members' copyright enabling users to search and download files from other *Kazaa* users. In November 2001, the District Court of Amsterdam ruled that *Kazaa* breached the copyright law through facilitation of unlicensed sharing of protected works and ordered its administrators to take such measures as to prevent further copyright infringement of the *Buma/Stemra* repertoire, even if is necessary to close *Kazaa* website.[60] In addition, it was held that the decision would not be restricted only to the Netherlands because of the global character of Internet. For the Court was sufficient that *Kazaa* software allowed file sharing to be performed and the fact that, unlike Napster, *Kazza* P2P network did not operate a central server was irrelevant. However,

---

[59] H. Hartwig, "Online auctioneers must work harder in Germany", Bardehle Pagenberg Publications (2004).
[60] *Kazaa v. Buma/Stemra* KG 01/2264 OdC, Amsterdam District Court (29 November 2001).

reversing the District Court's Decision, the Court of Appeals dismissed *Kazaa*'s secondary liability as concluded that it was impossible for *Kazaa* to control the transfer of infringing files via its own file sharing network, as well as to identify those files which were protected by copyright, and even the closing down of *Kazaa* would not prevent this illegal activity.[61] It was also found that not *Kazaa*, but its users have carried infringing acts.

However, in later cases, which involved a request for an order towards ISPs to disconnect P2P copyright infringing websites, the District Court's decision was confirmed. First, in *Stichting BREIN v. KPN*[62] the Court found that an owner of P2P BitTorrent site acted wrongfully "not because the website owner was infringing the copyrights or neighbouring rights vested in rightful owners, but because his actions conflicted with the due care to observe towards the rightful owners"[63] and thus he facilitated structural copyright infringement. Similarly, in *Stichting BREIN v. Leaseweb BV*[64] without to make a decision at preliminary injunction stage whether *Everlasting*'s website infringed the copyright, the Dutch court found that defendant's BitTorrent site "structurally facilitated the infringement of copyrights and neighbouring rights and the website owner must be aware of this. *Everlasting*'s conduct therefore is unlawful, because it is contrary to the principle of due care that must be observed *vis-à-vis* those entitled to copyright".[65]

---

[61] *Kazaa v. Buma/Stemra* No 1370/01 SKG, Court of Appeals, Netherlands (28 March 2002). Later, the decision was upheld by the Netherlands Supreme Courts.
[62] No 276747, Hague Court, Netherlands (5 January 2007).
[63] Ibid., at para. 4.4.
[64] No 369220/KG ZA 07-850 AB/MB, Amsterdam District Court (27 June 2007). Later, the decision was upheld by Amsterdam Court of Appeals.
[65] Ibid., at para. 5.4.

Between January 2007 and June 2009 the German collecting society *GEMA* brought legal proceedings against the file sharing service *RapidShare* before various courts within the country. The P2P network in question offered a virtual storage space, allowing users to upload content on it and thus making the respective copyright material available to the public. According to GEMA, *RapidShare* has made about 15 million files available to its users without obtaining licence. In January 2007, the District Court of Cologne granted a temporary injunction against the defendant although he claimed to have no actual knowledge and control of the content uploaded and therefore no legal liability. By its injunction the Court has made it clear that a mere circumstance of shifting acts of use and the purported inability of the P2P network operator to supervise content onto its website, from legal point of view, did not relieve the operator in question from copyright liability which he possesses for infringements occurred within the context of its file sharing service.[66] Similarly, in January 2008, the Regional Court of Dusseldorf ruled that *RapidShare* was responsible for the copyright content uploaded and downloaded by its clients and if the defendant fails to take appropriate measures against the transfer of copyright protected material in future, it will be required to pay severe damages. It was irrelevant whether such measures will render its business model much less attractive or even entirely suspended.[67] The

---

[66] GEMA Press Release January 2007 (www.gema.de/en/press/press-releases); R. W. Smith, "GEMA obtains injunctions against data exchange services", Berlin January 2007.
[67] GEMA Press Release January 2008 (www.gema.de/en/press/press-releases); J. Cheng, "No safe harbour for RapidShare in copyright infringement case", USA January 2008.

latest episode of *GEMA – RapidShare* legal saga took place between October 2008 and June 2009 where the Regional Court of Hamburg stated that the owners of *RapidShare* must implement effective filtering system to avoid copyright liability. Despite the fact that defendant has already imputed such system based on a hash filter technology and engaged six full time employees to remove the infringing files, the German court found those measures not efficiently enough because any file could be changed with just a few bytes in order to bypass the filter and therefore *RapidShare* should check the content on its website for copyright infringement before it is published or made available on Internet, as well as to log the IP addresses of alleged infringers.[68] In addition, the *RapidShare* owner's argument that it was impossible for him to stay in business if he would have to check every single file was rejected on the grounds that "a business model that does not use common methods of prevention cannot claim protection of the law."[69] Furthermore, *GEMA* was granted with a court order requiring *RapidShare* to block 5 000 songs belonged to its members.

In June 2008, the Court of Appeals of Turku (Finland) affirmed the decision of the District Court which held the BitTorent based P2P network *Finreactor* as illegal and its operators liable for users' copyright infringing acts.[70] The legal proceedings involved several plaintiffs, such as *Twentieth Century Fox*, *Walt Disney*

---

[68] GEMA Press Release June 2009 (www.gema.de/en/press/press-releases); N. Anderson, "Achtung! RapidShare ordered to filter all user uploads", USA, June 2009.
[69] Ibid.
[70] Mikko Manner, "A Bittorrent P2P Network Shut Down and Its Operation Deemed Illegal in Finland" [2009] Ent.L.R. 20(1), 21–24.

and *Microsoft*, and more than 30 defendants. According to the charges filed in the case, *Finreactor* had more than 10 000 users and the combined value of unauthorised copyright works acquired was approximately several million Euros. It is worth pointing that the *Finreactor*'s operators were prosecuted under the Finish Penal Code[71] for criminal copyright infringement or alternatively for civil copyright violation, namely for damages and financial loss suffered by the plaintiffs. *Finreactor*'s administrators claimed that their service amounted merely to database consisting of hyperlinks to copyright material. Defendants argued that the content was transmitted directly between users and since the infringements had actually not taken place within the *Finreactor* service itself, they had no any legal responsibility. Considering the P2P network as a whole, the Finish court found that defendants had participated in copyright infringements or aiding and abetting thereto due to the maintenance and continuous development of *Finreactor* system and therefore evidentially and undisputable they had been aware of the infringing uses and behaviour. Additionally, before the Court of Appeal *Finreactor*'s administrators claimed that their network was in fact an information society service as defined in the Finish Act on the Provision of Information Society Services based on the EU E-Commerce Directive and hence the failure of plaintiffs to file a takedown notice has released the defendants of any financial liability for possible copyright infringements occurred on *Finreactor* file sharing service. This argument was rejected on the grounds that aforementioned provisions did not apply to this case "since the defendants also participated in the provision of the

---

[71] Finish Penal Code, Chapter 49 Violation of certain incorporeal rights, s.1 Copyright offence.

content of the service as administrators of the service and thus the exemption from liability was not applicable."[72] Whereas the Court concluded that the essential elements of criminal copyright infringement were not fulfilled because there was no clear intent for financial benefit, it found administrators guilty for copyright violation and ordered them to pay over EUR 420 000 as damages and over EUR 142 000 as legal expenses to the copyright holders.

In April, the same year the District Court of Stockholm (Sweden) held the four founders and administrators of the most famous worldwide file sharing website *The Pirate Bay*[73] liable for secondary copyright infringement.[74] *The Pirate Bay* case has resembled strongly *Finreactor* case, namely the type of P2P network involved was the same; similarly, the legal proceeding were brought under both criminal copyright infringement offence and civil claims for damages; the defence was based on the same arguments; and the Swedish court found secondary civil liability in the same manner. By reason of that defendants were ordered to pay damages amounted to EUR 2.7 million to *Sony Music*, *Warner Bros*, *EMI* and *Columbia Pictures* for infringing their movies, music and gaming titles. However, unlike *Finreactor* case, each of the *The Pirate Bay*'s operators was sentenced to one year in prison. Under the Swedish Penal Code[75] and

---

[72] Mikko Manner, "A Bittorrent P2P Network Shut Down and Its Operation Deemed Illegal in Finland" [2009] Ent.L.R. 20(1), 21–24.
[73] With over 3.5million registered users, 22 million users in total and a self-proclaimed status of "the world's largest BitTorrent tracker" (www.thepiratebay.org); currently claiming over 150 million users (www.bittorrent.com).
[74] Docket no. B 13301-06, Stockholm District Court, Sweden (17 April 2009).
[75] Swedish Penal Code Ds 1999:36, as amended.

Copyright Act[76] the prosecutor authority sought together with the plaintiffs an imposition of criminal liability for contributions to copyright offence and civil liability for damages covering the financial loss suffered respectively.[77] To establish a criminal liability under Swedish law, it has to be proved that defendants had been aware of the infringements, had with their acts contributed to the copyright infringements and had intended to earn financial benefit from the file sharing network.[78] The Court found the four defendants liable for criminal copyright offence in relation to all grounds. Firstly, it reached the conclusion that *The Pirate Bay*'s administrators had been aware of the fact that the exchange of copyright works was facilitated by their website. Secondly, "by providing a website with ... well-developed search functions, easy uploading and storage possibilities, and with a tracker linked to the website, the accused have incited the crimes that the file sharers have committed".[79] And thirdly, by "extensive accessibility of others' copyrights and the fact that the operation was conducted commercially and in an organised fashion"[80] the defendants had gained a financial advantage of the illegal uploading and downloading performed on their P2P network. In regard to allegation that the safe harbours under the Swedish Act on Electronic Commerce based on the EU E-Commerce Directive[81] were applicable to *The Pirate Bay* the

---

[76] Swedish Copyright Act SFS 1960:729, as amended
[77] As it has already pointed the Court's findings in relation to the civil liability were the same as in *Finreactor* case and thereupon only the criminal part of the legal proceedings will be discussed in details.
[78] M. Manner, T. Siniketo & U. Polland, "The Pirate Bay Ruling – When the fun and games end" [2009] Ent. L.R. 201.
[79] Docket no. B 13301-06, Stockholm District Court, Sweden (17 April 2009).
[80] Ibid.
[81] Directive 2000/31/EC, Art.12 (Mere Conduit Defence), Art.13 (Caching Defence) and Art.14 (Hosting Defence).

District Court stated that a service where user could upload and store torrent files on a website may be considered as hosting service in accordance with Article 14 of the Directive, but as such *The Pirate Bay*'s file sharing network did not fulfil the conditions laid down in the provision that upon obtaining knowledge of infringing activity the service provider must expeditiously remove or disable the access to any illegal content.[82] Therefore the defendant's claim was rejected.

The legal fight between entertainment industry and *The Pirate Bay* still continues across Europe. In July 2009, the District Court of Amsterdam ruled that *The Pirate Bay*'s administrators must stop all its activities in the Netherlands within ten days and to pay damages of EUR 30 000 per day up to a maximum of EUR 3 million in total, if they do not comply with Court's decision. The legal proceedings were brought by *Stichting BREIN*[83] claiming that *The Pirate Bay* BitTorrent service was responsible for millions of copyright infringements every day and therefore it should be blocked for any users in the Netherlands. In August 2009, *FIMI* and *FPM*[84] announced that they have filed a civil case under the Italian law against the founders of *The Pirate Bay* calming for damages in excess of EUR 1 million. The same month *AIMR*[85] began a legal action against a Romanian P2P network carrying a large backup of *The Pirate Bay*.

---

[82] Ibid., Art. 14(1)(b).
[83] Stichting BREIN – Protection Entertainment Rights Industry of the Netherlands
[84] FIMI – Italian Federation of the Music Industry; FPM – The Italian Federation against Musical Piracy.
[85] AIMR – Romanian Association of the Music Industry.

In August 2009, the District Court of Utrecht (the Netherlands) ordered the Dutch based P2P network *Mininova* to remove all torrent files linking to plaintiffs' copyright works within three months or to pay damages of EUR 1000 per day up to maximum of EUR 5 million.[86] With over 30 million visitors per month *Mininova* was one of the largest BittTorent file sharing website, which have displayed torrents submitted by its clients and carried legitimate premium content from publishers, such as *Canadian Broadcasting Corporation*. Similarly to *RapidShare* case in Germany, the Court found that *Mininova* had not implemented effective measures to protect the copyright of *Stichting BREIN*'s members even thought *Mininova*'s owners launched a copyright filtering system together with *Motion Picture Association* and employed several moderators to remove torrents that link to adult content, viruses and fake files. It should be noted that the plaintiffs' claim was not directed to the closing down of *Mininova* P2P network, but to the filtering technology implemented which was based on infringing keywords and digital fingerprints.

Lastly, it is worth pointing the controversial ruling of the Mercantile Court of Barcelona (Spain) from July 2009. Rejecting *SAGE*'s[87] request for precautionary measures against the file sharing network *Elrincondejesus*, the Court stated that "P2P networks, as mere networks for transfer of data between Internet users, does not, in principle, breach any rights protected by the Spanish Intellectual Property Act".[88] In regard to the

---

[86] K. Fiveash, "*Mininova* flattened by Dutch court", EPM Newsletter, the Netherlands, August 2009.
[87] SAGE – Spanish Society of Authors, Composers and Publishers.
[88] *SAGE v. Elrincondejesus*, Mercantile Court No 7, Barcelona, Judge Raul N. Garcia (2 July 2007).

possible copyright infringement, it was held that uploading of work on a P2P website that previously has been converted in combatable computer file, does not amount to an act of reproduction. In addition, the subsequent downloading was considered as non-commercial copying or "collective use, such as broadcasting in a store."[89] Additionally, the Spanish Court found that the Act describes distribution as requiring something tangible, which does not exist in the transmission via on-line file sharing network. Furthermore, the Court concluded that even if a public distribution was occurred, it would be very difficult to prove it due to the possibility for the files to be shared with just one single person.[90]

Generally, it can be seen that European national courts may held liable file sharing software providers who do more than a mere provision of facilities used by others to infringe copyright holders' rights. A secondary liability could be applied in cases where defendant has actively encouraged infringing acts and subsequently, has benefited financially from such illegal use. Additionally, if P2P network distributors have failed to adopt any available technological measures when they became aware of any infringing use of their services or the measures implemented have not been effective, then they would not escape the imposition of indirect copyright infringement. It can be noted that the elements of defendant's knowledge about users' infringing conducts, similarly to the Commonwealth authorisation doctrine, have not been interpreted literally. The courts in aforementioned European civil law jurisdiction have construed the notion of

---

[89] Ibid.
[90] The full trial will take place at a later date.

knowledge to comprise situations where P2P network providers should have known about the infringement or should have known about the likely infringing behaviour of others and as a result of that the third party in question owed a duty of care not to assist or abet others in such illegal activity. Furthermore, the duty of due care was extended to implementation of efficient filtering technological measures to prevent existing and future copyright infringement, as well as to acts of "blinding oneself to infringement".[91] Therefore, it can be said that copyright holders and their representatives could sue successfully the distributors of P2P software without having to chase the end users instead.

However, it can be pointed out that there is still uncertainty within Europe in relation to indirect copyright infringement. In *Buma/Stemra* case the secondary liability was dismissed by the Court of Appeals on the grounds that it was not possible for *Kazaa* to recognise which from the shared files contained copyright material and thus to control their illegal transfer. As it was seen in the second chapter, in countries with strong private copyright exception, such as France, the Court found the use of P2P file sharing network legal, as far as it is directed for personal rather than commercial purposes.[92] In regard to primary infringement Spain had implemented the WIPO Treaties and EU Directives and under its intellectual property law unauthorised file sharing is unlawful. Accordingly, the private copy exception is irrelevant in cases where file sharing service is involved and thus

---

[91] A. N. Dixon, "Liability of users and third parties for copyright infringements on the internet: overview of international developments" (*Peer-to-peer file sharing and secondary liability in copyright law* edited by A. Strowel, Edward Elgar 2009), at page 38.
[92] *Société Civile des Producteurs Phonographiques v. Anthony G* 31 chambre/2 (8 December 2005).

users caught to exchange files even for personal use should be subject to civil charges. Furthermore similarly to other European civil law countries, there is a general principle under Spanish Civil Code which imposes liability to someone who through his negligence or fault causes harm.[93] Consequently, it seems logical a secondary liability to be imposed on a P2P network provider, who by promoting its software infringes someone else's copyright. However, under a Spanish law the existence of specific-related law usually prevails over and renders the general civil rules inapplicable. Therefore, the application of third party's liability in the field of on-line file sharing could be possible if it was laid down expressly under the Intellectual Property Act.[94] The lack of such provision was enough for the Court in *SAGE* case to establish a presumption of innocence in relation to P2P activities.

In contrast, under the Finish and Swedish law, both civil and criminal liability for indirect copyright infringement have been implemented and have been applied in events where a file sharing service was used to make available unauthorised copyright material. *Finreactor* and *The Pirate Bay*'s decisions have placed a high threshold for the safe harbour provisions to P2P network administrators. Even the considerably technical and complex nature of BitTorent file sharing systems could not prevent the imposition of secondary criminal liability and thus, the issue was whether the acts of P2P software distributors were criminal "aiding" or "preparation" to users' copyright

---

[93] Spanish Civil Code, Art. 1902.
[94] M. Daly, "Life after *Grokster*: analysis of US and European approaches to file sharing" [2007] EIPR, 29(8), 319-324.

infringement. In *The Pirate Bay* case the court held the aiding theory, but dismissed the preparation, which respectively would have resulted in less civil damages and shorter sentence. However, the criminal law doctrines to indirect copyright infringements in Europe are still not harmonised and as a result, a P2P network operator may be held liable under the Finnish or Swedish criminal law but may escape liability according to the criminal law of other Member States.[95]

---

[95] As it was pointed in second chapter the adoption of EU Directive on criminal measures aimed at ensuring the enforcement of intellectual property rights is still pending.

4. ROLE AND LIABILITY OF INTERNET SERVICE PROVIDERS

4.1 EU E-Commerce Directive

As it can be seen end users and P2P software providers have a main role in the illegal file sharing on Internet. However, this process involves another important participant, namely the Internet service providers (ISPs). The question for the role and liability of ISPs has been raised in both legislative and litigation contexts. Usually, Internet services are provided by major telecommunications companies and their initial demands for specific statutory exceptions to an intermediary liability for Internet related telecommunications activities had been satisfied to certain extend throughout the world. It is accepted that a mere provision of physical facilities as such does not make the ISPs liable for communication (transfer, transmission, exchange or sharing) of copyright material conducted by others.[96] In Europe these ISPs liability statutory exceptions, also known as safe harbours or shelters, have been implemented by the EU E-Commerce Directive.

Before the introduction of the Directive in *Hi Bit Software v. AOL Bertelsmann Online*[97] a secondary liability for users' unlawful acts was applied to a German ISP. The plaintiffs who have distributed digital recordings of songs used by performers as backing tracks sued *AOL Bertelsmann Online* for copyright infringement by allowing the recordings in question to be downloaded from its

---

[96] Agreed Statements Concerning Article 8, WIPO Copyright Treaty. See *note* 19.
[97] [2002] ECDR 27 (8 March 2001).

website. The District Court of Munich concluded that whereas knowledge about the illegal copyright files being downloaded was within the competence of the ISP due to the use of text editors to open files, no such knowledge could be imposed to the uploading of copyright materials. However, rejecting the lower court's findings, the Court of Appeals held that the defendant had facilitated the transfer of musical works between its clients and thus his conduct "amounted in general and with regard to the titles which are the subject matter of the dispute to gross negligence, if not even eventual intent".[98] Additionally, it was stated that liability would not be raised if an ISP merely hosts content without any knowledge of infringing copyright material or acts promptly to disable access when became aware of such illegal material. Likewise, the French case law put distinction between a defendant who hosts content and a defendant who provides links to copyright material stored elsewhere.[99] Furthermore, the Court of Appeals in the Hague (Netherlands) dismissed copyright infringement actions against an ISP on the grounds that as a host the defendant only provided technical facilities for others to exchange information.[100]

The European Commission' attempts to promote either general or limited immunities to telecommunications and internet service providers eventually led to the introduction of the EU E-Commerce Directive. The Directive offers several defences to the

---

[98] Ibid., at 38.
[99] *Perathoner v. S. Joseph Societe Free* [2003] ECDR 8 (23 May 2001).
[100] *Church of Spiritual Technology v. Dataweb BV* [2004] ECDR 25 (4 September 2003). The Court referred to Agreed Statements Concerning Article 8, WIPO Copyright Treaty.

ISPs, which have already been implemented into the national laws of Member States. Firstly, an ISP will not be liable for information transmitted through the use of its service where the ISP does not initiate the transmission, does not select the receiver of the transmission and does not expressly modify the information of the transmission.[101] Secondly, there is no liability for an automatic, intermediate and temporary storage of information for the sole purpose of more efficient onwards transmission.[102] Thirdly, an ISP will not be liable for storing information provided it has no actual knowledge of illegal activity and upon obtaining such knowledge, the ISP, in order to avoid liability, expeditiously removes or disables access to the information in question.[103] It can be noted that the purpose of the Directive is to provide some form of protection against claims that ISPs may be liable for violation of copyright by transmitting, cashing or storing illegal audio-visual works. However, the secondary liability approaches noted in the previous chapter do not release ISPs from certain due care requirements or limitations which, according to European national courts, comprise activities such as filtering and blocking of P2P network providers and users involved in unauthorised transfer of copyright material, as well as disclosing the identity of Internet subscribers.

---

[101] Directive 2000/31/EC., Art.12 (Mere Conduit Defence).
[102] Ibid., Art.13 (Caching Defence).
[103] Ibid., Art.14 (Hosting Defence).

4.2 Filtering and blocking

The EU Directives allow injunctions requiring ISPs to filter or block infringing content or acts of websites and users on its network, even without the finding that the ISPs themselves are liable for copyright infringement.[104] Such third party injunctions have been adopted willingly by national courts in Europe in their attempts to suspend illegal copyright activities on Internet. Likewise, in Denmark the Supreme Court ordered the country's largest telecommunications provider to cut off the Internet connection of two individuals who had offered infringing music files via the ISP's network.[105] According to the Court, "failure to impose such an injunction would violate Article 8(3) of the EU Copyright Directive".[106] In *IFPI Danmark v. Tele2*[107] the City Court of Copenhagen found that both the Russia-based file sharing service *allofmp3.com* by offering for download unauthorised music to the ISP's Danish subscribers and the ISP itself by transmitting this illegal content had infringed the plaintiff's copyright. As a result, the court issued a targeted injunction requiring *Tele2* to block the access to the Russian P2P website. Similarly, in February 2009, the same ISP was ordered to block the access to *The Pirate Bay*'s domains in Denmark.[108] It was held that *Tele2* had contributed to the illegal exchange of copyright material, even though it had not been directly liable for it.[109] It can be noted that the Danish courts has established

---

[104] EU Copyright Directive 2001/29/EC, Art. 8(3); EU Commerce Directive 2000/31/EC, recitals 40 and 45.
[105] *IFPI v. TDC* Case No U2006.1474H, Danish Supreme Court (10 February 2006).
[106] Ibid.
[107] Case No FI15124/2006, Copenhagen City Court (25 October 2006).
[108] *IFPI v. DMT2/Tele2* Case No FS 14324/2007 (5 February 2008).

consistent approach in regard to the imposition of indirect copyright infringement to ISPs. According to it, an ISP may be held liable for temporary storage of infringing data in their routers and to be forced to block websites and users' Internet accounts that are mainly used to spread unlawful content.

In other European jurisdictions the courts had adopted injunctions covering particular on-line copyright infringers in a similar manner. In the Netherlands, the Court ordered an ISP to remove a P2P BitTorrent network from its server on the grounds that it would breach its own duty of due care by not removing client's file sharing website.[110] Likewise, the Swedish ISP *Black Internet* was obliged by Court's injunction to disconnect *The Pirate Bay* from Internet.[111] In France an ISP was ordered to suspend more than 100 customers' Internet accounts found to be engaged in unauthorised file sharing.[112] Moreover, the Finish leading ISP *TeliaSonera*, following the Court's injunction, cut off the internet connection of individual who was uploading a significant amount of infringing music files.[113]

Whereas third party injunctions are expected right holders' tool against Internet piracy, a recent case in Belgium have shown the willingness of the Court to require implementation of

---

[109] Oscar Swartz, "Denmark and The Pirate Bay: Take it to the European Court of Justice", Sweden, February 2008.
[110] *Stichting BREIN v. KPN* No 276747, Hague Court, Netherlands (5 January 2007); *Stichting BREIN v. Leaseweb* No 369220/KG ZA 07-850 AB/MB, Amsterdam District Court (27 June 2007).
[111] IFPI Chez Republic Press Release (http://www.ifpicr.cz/?rubrika=1197), Stockholm District Court (24 August 2009).
[112] IFPI Pres Release 4 April 2006 (http://www.ifpi.org/site-content/press/20060404a.html).
[113] IFPI Digital Music Report, January 2009 (http://www.ifpi.org/content/section_resources/dmr2009.html).

considerably broad filtering of the Internet traffic. In *SABAM v. SA Scarlet*[114] the Belgian collecting society of musical producers sought and obtained an injunction requiring the ISP *Scarlet* to implement technical measures in order to prohibit its subscribers from unauthorised transmission through P2P networks of any files containing musical works represented by the plaintiffs. It is worth pointing that defendant was ordered to prevent illegal file sharing not from certain P2P applications within its service, but from all P2P applications available on its network. Following the analysis by the experts appointed,[115] it was decided that the implementation of filtering technology could recognise 90 per cent of illegal music files shared on Internet and deal with defendant's large volume of Internet traffic.[116] The Belgian court rejected *Scarlet*'s objection that such duty amounts to general obligations to monitor the global network, which is contrary to EU E-Commerce Directive. In addition, it was held that the cost of installation of the filtering system ultimately payable by the users, would not be excessive and thus economically justifiable. The Court concluded that such injunction do not impose liability on the ISP and do not "violate the right of confidential correspondence or freedom of expression".[117]

It is clear that Internet users who have distributed audio-visual works without permission from right holders have committed copyright infringement. The fundamental issue, however, is to

---

[114] Cardozo Arts & Entertainment Journal Translation Series #001, Case No 04/8975, Brussels District Court (29 June 2007).
[115] The expert presented 11 solutions that could be applied in order to block or filter the file-sharing, and seven of them could be applied by *Scarlet*.
[116] The decision must be implemented in 6 months or the ISP must pay EUR 2 500 per day as damages for non-compliance.
[117] Ibid., at page 1289.

what extent the ISPs could be forced to block and filter those illegal activities. Upon obtaining knowledge of infringing activity a service providers must expeditiously remove or disable the access to illegal content.[118] Therefore, Court's injunctions requiring ISPs to block copyright infringing websites and subscribers are in accordance with the EU E-Commerce directive. On other hand, the Directive is intended to distinguish ISPs from software distributors who provide, operate and encourage file sharing activities. Unlike ISPs, such P2P network providers could not benefit from the safe harbours of the Directive and have obligation to monitor their services for illegal exchange of copyright material by its clients. The *SABAM* decision, by imposing broad surveillance duty on the ISP, equals both business models and somewhat ignores the distinction between them laid down in the EU E-Commerce Directive. In addition, if there is an evidence of some workable technical solution, the ISPs should not only apply it, but they have to charge the users for its installation. Hence, the copyright holders would place unjustifiably the price for protection of their works to the customers.[119] Furthermore, telecommunications companies have argued that such filtering technology would affect the legitimate transfer via Internet and, respectively, the lawful users' activities. Likewise, if ISPs' routers (nodes) are considered as committing copyright infringement as soon as unauthorised material passes between two or more of them, then the Internet traffic would be virtually impossible due to the liability for copyright infringement which each Internet account will possess.[120]

---

[118] Directive 2000/31/EC, Art. 14(1)(b).
[119] R. Clark, "Sharing out online liability: sharing files, sharing risks and targeting ISPs" (*Peer-to-peer file sharing and secondary liability in copyright law* edited by A. Strowel, Edward Elgar 2009), at page 228.

4.3 Discovery of identity orders

The identity of Internet users who have been involved in illegal file sharing activities is initially unknown to the right holders. In order to bring legal proceedings against file sharers, copyright holders should formulate legal grounds upon how to obtain the infringers' name and address from ISPs. The EU Data Protection Directive[121] and the EU Telecommunications Protection Directive[122] afford privacy protections for subscribers who have contracted with particular ISP. However, such privacy protections may be restricted with "appropriate and proportionate measure within a democratic society to safeguard ... the investigation, detection and prosecution of criminal offences..."[123] A dispute arises when European national courts, considering the EU Enforcement Directive, have to decide whether they have the power to compel ISPs to disclose the identity of its clients in civil legal proceedings. In *BREIN v. UPC Nederlands (Chello)*[124] the plaintiffs together with fifty records companies sought discovery of identity order against five Dutch ISPs in respect to file sharers whose IP addresses were allocated within the service of ISPs in question. The District Court of Utrecht found that the Dutch Civil Code,[125]

---

[120] Oscar Swartz, "Denmark and The Pirate Bay: Take it to the European Court of Justice", Sweden, February 2008.

[121] Directive 95/46/EC of the European Parliament and of the Council of 24 October 1995 on the protection of individuals with regard to the processing of personal data and on the free movement of such data [1995] OJ L281/11.

[122] Directive 2002/58/EC of the European Parliament and of the Council of 12 July 2002 concerning the processing of personal data and the protection of privacy in the electronic communications sector (Directive on privacy and electronic communications) [2002] OJ L201 /7.

[123] Ibid., Art. 15(1).

[124] Case No 194741/KGZA-05-462/BL/EV, Utrecht District Court (12 July 2005).

[125] Dutch Civil Code, Art. 6:196c.

as well as the EU E-Commerce Directive and the EU Enforcement Directive, required a general duty for disclosure due to the social obligation of due care that a service provider must bear in mind. However, the Court rejected to issue an order on the basis of several factors. Firstly, in order to indentify the possible infringers *BREIN* had employed the American company *MediaSentry*, which had not signed the EU/US Safe Harbour Agreement.[126] Additionally, it was found that the United States could not be considered as a country with fitting level of data protection. Therefore, the investigation and collection of IP addresses by this overseas party was held unlawful and respectively, the result of such activities could not be used to obtain user's information from the ISP. Secondly, the plaintiffs had not applied for a special license before the Dutch Data Protection Authority. And thirdly, the software used was not sophisticated enough to identify the infringing acts and there was a possibility wrong users to be subject of the claims. Further, the Dutch Supreme Court in *Lycos v. Pessers*[127] continued to explore the extent of the ISPs' general duty for disclosure and laid down four criteria, which must be fulfilled for a successful discovery of identity order. Firstly, it must be sufficiently plausible that the information is unlawful against the third party; secondly, the third party must have a genuine interest in obtaining the personal data; thirdly, it must be plausible that there are no other less drastic method to obtain the information; and fourthly, the interests of the third party, of the ISP and of the user must

---

[126] US-EU Safe Harbour Agreement regarding personal data collected in the European Economic Area, July 2000.
[127] Danish Supreme Court (25 November 2005); A. Roosendaal, "Elimination of Anonymity in regard to Liability for Unlawful Acts on the Internet" Tilburg University, the Netherlands 2005 (http://arno.uvt.nl/show.cgi?fid=94167).

be weighted and the third party's interest must prevail. Subsequently, the Court concluded that these requirements were fulfilled and ordered the defendant to reveal the name and address of its subscriber.

Data protection legislation in the United Kingdom and Ireland allows personal information to be obtained following Court's order.[128] Civil procedural rules of discovery were established in *Norwich Pharmacal v. Customs and Excise Commissioners*[129] where the House of Lords held that a person who, even innocently, gets involved in infringing acts is obliged to assist to the injury party by providing the identity of the direct infringer and other vital information. Accordingly, in *EMI Records v. Eircom*[130] the Irish High Court granted an order against the defendant in respect to seventeen file sharers. The Court found that the demonstration of infringing activity, prejudicial to *EMI*'s copyright, must prevail over the right of privacy or confidentiality. However, it was stated that the information obtained in the course of the legal proceedings could be used only in copyright infringement proceedings in Ireland and could not be transferred to other national jurisdictions.

In Austria, an ISP was ordered by the Court of Appeals of Vienna to reveal personal information of its user who was charged with offering for download on Internet of several thousand illegal music files. Considering the Austrian statutory provision, the Court found that the disclosure of user' personal data will provide

---

[128] UK Data Protection Act 1988, s. 35; Irish Data Protection Act, s. 8(e).
[129] [1974] AC 133.
[130] [2006] ECDR 5.

evidence of illegal actions to the materially interested third party; therefore such discovery is legitimately required.[131] Similarly, in June 2009, the District Court of Solna (Sweden) ordered the ISP *Ephone* to disclose the name and addresses of several subscribers engaged in unauthorised file sharing.[132]

Recent decisions in Italy have favoured copyright holders too. The German record company *Peppermint* was successful in granting discovery of identity order in two separate legal proceedings against the Italian ISPs *Wind* and *Telecom Italia* on the grounds that the data protection legislature permits disclosure in courts in order for the plaintiffs to protected their rights against possible damages in fastest possible way and delaying plaintiffs' request would cause unfair damage to them.[133] However, in February 2008, the Italian Data Protection Authority held as unlawful the use of software by private companies designed to identify users who exchange copyright material via P2P networks.[134] It was concluded that monitoring and data collection amount to interception or surveillance which is forbidden to private parties under Article 122 of the Italian Data Protection Code and Article 5 of the EU Telecommunications Protection Directive and therefore *Peppermint* was ordered to erase any personal data by the end of March 2008.[135]

---

[131] A. van Beelen, "The name behind the number" DLA Piper Publications, Amsterdam, December 2005.
[132] "Publishers win anti- piracy law test case" The Local Sweden's News in English, 25 June 2009
(http://www.thelocal.se/20274/20090625/).
[133] E. Prosperetti, "The Peppermint "Jam": peer-to-peer goes to court in Italy" [2008] Ent. L.R. 18(8), 280-283.
[134] Previously, by investigating the software company *Logistep* which was employed by *Peppermint* to identify the private IP addresses of alleged infringers, Swiss Data Protection Authority has come to same conclusion.
[135] A. Arena, "Monitoring the Activities of P2P Users Runs Foul of Privacy

In France, the national Data Protection Authority rejected an automated surveillance of users of file sharing systems because "it did not put in place a system of one-off actions strictly limited to the needs of fighting Internet piracy but could lead, on the contrary, in a mass collection of online personal data and in an extensive and constant surveillance of P2P networks."[136] However, the decision was overruled by the Supreme Court, which considering the importance of digital piracy, found that proposed system for collecting evidence of illegal file-sharing was not disproportionate.[137] In addition, the Court acknowledged that ISPs were not entitled to use their subscribers' personal information to send educational messages on behalf of third parties, such as collecting societies.

In contrast, the German prosecutor authorities and courts have clearly rejected music industry's demands to order ISPs to disclose personal data of users suspected in illegal file sharing. In October 2006, the chief public prosecutor's office in Berlin accused copyright holders[138] of trying "under the cover of pretending to initiate criminal proceedings to obtain for free by exploiting the limited resources of prosecuting authorities and at the expense of the budget of the federal state of Berlin a personal data required for successful pursuit of civil claims".[139] In

Legislation" IRIS Legal Observations of the European Audiovisual Observatory, July 2008.
[136] CNIL decision, 24 October 2005, (http://www.cnil.fr/english); N. Jondet, "French Supreme Court allows tracking of P2P users" French Law in English, June 2007 (http://french-law.net/french-supreme-court-allows-tracking-of-p2p-users-ce-23-mai-2007.html).
[137] French Supreme Court, Case No 288149 (23 May 2007).
[138] Specially the law firm Schutt-Waetke which had filed compliants on massive scale asking for the indentifications of 9,186 IP addresses

July 2007, the Local Court of Offenburg held a discovery of identity order as disproportionate on the grounds that plaintiffs failed to show how the alleged offenders had been engaged in acts that had created a criminally relevant damage.[140] Likewise, European Court of Justice in *Productores de Musica de Espana Promusicae v. Telefonica de Espana*[141] distinguished civil legal proceedings from criminal investigations or matters of public security and national defence. It was ruled that under the EU Directives the national courts are not obliged to compel ISPs to reveal personal information relating to individual users for the purposes of civil proceedings.[142] However, the Court stated that the Member States are not necessarily precluded from introducing laws to that effect due to the relatively general character of the EU legislature since it has to be applied to a large number of various situations which may arise under any national jurisdictions.[143]

It can be seen that Dutch and Irish courts perceived the unlawful exchange via P2P networks to such serious threat to intellectual property rights so as to require the subordination of personal data protection even in civil legal proceedings and thus, to secure effectively the interests of copyright holders. However, as a result from the courts' decisions in Netherlands and Ireland, as well as in Austria and Sweden, it can be concluded that the right

---

[139] R. W. Smith, "Public prosecutors refuse to collect IP address-related information from providers" Heise On-line Magazine, Berlin August 2007 (http://www.heise.de/english/newsticker/news/93759).
[140] Ibid.,
[141] Case C-275/06 [2008] ECDR.
[142] Ibid., at [70].
[143] Ibid., at [67].

to operate an ISP includes the observance of duty of care, which is far from the immunities for such telecommunications activity laid down in the EU E-Commerce Directive. Hence, this could lead to loss of existing and future subscribers, who in order to escape copyright infringement and exposure of their personal data would contract with other ISPs, as well as to continuous change of IP addresses and massive use of technology and software for avoiding detection, such as firewalls.[144]

The opposite decisions of Italian and French public authority and courts under their own national legislatures illustrated the high degree of confusion in relation to the safe harbours of the EU E-Commerce Directive, as well to the civil and criminal litigation. In Germany, it was recognised and rejected the practice of right holders to use factitious criminal procedural rules to compel a discovery of personal information relating to suspected infringers in order to succeed in civil claims. However, the European Court of Justice clarified the issue on discovery of identity orders as it held that national laws may be capable of being used to permit civil procedure to require an ISP to reveal users' personal data, but only through the prior implementation of specific legislature which derogates the requirement under the EU Telecommunications Protection Directive that ensures the confidentiality of personal information. Providing that there is no automatic right to disclosure such information, the decision certainly favours the ISPs.[145]

---

[144] R. Clark, "Sharing out online liability: sharing files, sharing risks and targeting ISPs" (*Peer-to-peer file sharing and secondary liability in copyright law* edited by A. Strowel, Edward Elgar 2009), at page 224.
[145] "L. Hetherington, "Peer-to-peer file sharing - ISPs and disclosure of user

5. POTENTIAL SOLUTIONS

5.1 Watermarking and encryption

A number of potential solutions to illegal on-line file sharing have been offered. The final chapter will be focused on two of them, namely watermarking and encryption, and private copyright levy. Digital rights management is term that refers to technological protection measures, such as watermarking and encryption, whose purpose is to permit secure access to copyright material in digital form and to enforce contractual licence agreements.[146] Watermarking and encryption enable right holders to restrict and control the access to their audio-visual works and their subsequent copies. Those techniques are broadly used in the online video and music stores. In each file available a key is incorporated comprising set of numbers which have to be matched in order for the copyright material to be downloaded or copied. By purchasing a licence, users obtain the matching combination of numbers that unlock the file and allows access to its copyright content. Controversial character of those access control techniques derives from the possibility in some cases for the technological control offered by them to go far beyond the protection allowed by copyright law. As a result, for instance, certain permitted actions such as private copying, may be prevented due to the restrictions implemented in the digital files.

---

identities" [2008] Ent. L.R. 19(4), 81-82.
[146] European Commission eYou Guide
(http://ec.europa.eu/information_society/eyouguide/fiches/glossary_ipr/index_en
.htm).

Legal protection of digital rights management technology in Europe has been implemented by the EU Information Society Directive. Provisions of the Directive have targeted both the acts of circumvention of the technological protection measures and the devices or products, including software, whose primary purpose is to enable or facilitate circumvention.[147] It can be said that the Directive clearly illustrates the broad extent to which the European legislature is prepared to go in providing legal defence to digital right management techniques, such as watermarking and encryption. However, the difficulty arises when these anti-circumvention provisions are applied to P2P networks. According to the Directive, liability should be imposed not just in relation to products primarily designed to enable and facilitate circumvention but also to devises promoted, advertised or marketed for the same purpose and to those which have only limited commercially purpose or use other than to circumvent.[148] On the other hand, notwithstanding the fact that file sharing services are used for illegal transfer of copyright material predominantly, there is always a possibility for non-infringing uses via them, as well as a chance for their advertisement and promotion for such lawful purposes. Therefore, in this situation the P2P networks could be considered legitimate and at the same time, as a software which circumvent the technology that locks up the files themselves, to infringe the anti-circumvention provisions.[149]

---

[147] Directive 2001/29/EC, Art. 6.
[148] Ibid., Art. 6(2).
[149] C. Nasir, "Taming the beast of file-sharing - legal and technological solutions to the problem of copyright infringement over the Internet: Part 1" [2005] Ent. L.R. 16(4), 82-88.

Availability of digital right management techniques had contributed to creation and growth of many lawful on-line stores. They offer to their customers an enormous variety of copyright works for a price similar to their physical counterparts and in some cases can generate sufficient profit to satisfy copyright holders.[150] However, most of Internet stores use their own confidential digital right management system, which does not allow for the files downloaded legitimately to be played or copied on every platform and thus, they restrict both the initial and subsequent copying. This could render difficult the access of files from different hardware and computer operating systems. In addition, by protecting copyright works themselves, right holders could obtain the control for their exploitation from the producers of playback and copying equipment. Furthermore, users of on-line stores are required to agree to extensive licence agreements reflecting the restrictions which anti-circumvention provisions enforce.

It can be said that despite the broad commercial application of watermarking and encryption technologies, their potential to prevent illegal file sharing and regulate Internet as a whole is restrained in several aspects. Firstly, the continuous development of anti-circumvention devises and software, as well as their increasing use, significantly endanger the existing technical protection measures. Secondly, the availability of one single unprotected copy could lead to its exponential spread throughout Internet and as a result, in order to be fully effective, the access

---

[150] For example, *ITunes Music* store of *Apple* and *eMusic* store have been commercially successful.

control technologies should be applied universally. Subsequently, this would restrict unduly the access to public domain works comprising partly copyright material and activities such as browsing documents and sampling music or films[151] and would create on-line environment where the use and spread of all creative content and information will be in digital lock-up.[152] Lastly, due to abovementioned restrictions a considerable part of users will prefer to obtain copies of protected works via such Internet technologies as Skype, e – mails and, of course, non-paid infringing P2P networks rather than to use the greater availability and legitimacy of paid file sharing websites and on-line stores.

5.2 Private copyright levy

Another potential solution to the illegal transfer of copyright material via P2P networks on Internet is the imposition of statutory licence that permits non-commercial file sharing in exchange of a levy that is aimed to compensate losses suffered by copyright holders. Such levy has for long time been an important instrument in balancing the authors' rights and public interests. Commonly known as a private copyright levy, this special tax or surcharge is applied additionally to any general sales tax on purchases of recordable media, such as blank CDs, DVDs, memory cards or coping equipment, such as computers, CD and DVD writers, music and video players and scanners. This

---

[151] C. Nasir, "Taming the beast of file-sharing - legal and technological solutions to the problem of copyright infringement over the Internet: Part 1" [2005] Ent. L.R. 16(4), 82-88.
[152] L. Lessig, *The Future of Ideas* Random House, New York (2001).

levy is paid by the manufacturers of those articles and thus its application does not distinguish the costumers who intend to use such media and equipment from those who do not. According to the proposed model, the private copyright levy will be paid from Internet users to ISPs, P2P network administrators or manufacturers of computers or playback devices where it will be passed to collecting societies or agencies and subsequently distributed to copyright holders.[153]

The extension of private copying levy in the digital sphere has received some support in Europe. It was argued that copyright in on-line environment should be replaced by levies because exclusive rights will either not be enforceable or their exercise will restrict the free flow of information on Internet.[154] Likewise, it was suggested that copyright on Internet should be transformed from an exclusive right to a mere remuneration right.[155] Accordingly, it would be preferable to permit a private copying exception as an enforceable right against technical protection devices and to solve the problem by a working system of equitable remuneration,[156] namely a mandatory collective administration of exclusive rights where collecting societies will be required to licence certain uses on a non-discriminating, fair basis.[157]

---

[153] N. W. Netanel, "Impose a Non-commercial Use Levy to Allow Free Peer-to-Peer File-Sharing" [2003] 17 Harvard Journal of Law and Technology 1, 19-22.

[154] P. Wittgenstein, *Die digitale Agenda der WIPO-Vertrage*, Bern Switzerland: Stampfli (2000).

[155] A. A. Wandtke, "Copyright und virtueller Markt in der Informationsgesellschaft" GRUG 49 (1), 7 (2002).

[156] C. Geiger, "Right to Copy v. Three-Step Test, „The Future of the Private Copy Exception in the Digital Environment" (2005) Computer Law Review International (1), 7.

[157] L. Guibault, *Copyright Limitations and Contracts: An Analysis of the*

As it was noted the implementation of private copyright levy system on copyright content exchanged via file sharing systems requires statutory licence, which would make all audio-visual works on Internet legally available. Subsequently, the quantity of material downloaded would be traced through combination of watermarking, sampling techniques and specialised arbitrations, controlled and monitored by administered collecting society. Therefore, the amount of levy would be ascertained on the basis of the quantity and nature of downloaded files. Furthermore, such model would be in accordance with the EU legislature[158] and the three-step test of the Bern Convention.[159]

On the other hand, the imposition of private copyright levy is itself a form of control of Internet access, which could raise a several enforcement issues. Firstly, by delegating their right to collecting societies, copyright holders could lose control over the

---

Contractual Overridability of Limitations on Copyright, Kluwer Law International (2002), at pages 26-27.

[158] Directive 2001/29/EC, Art. 5(2) "Member States may provide for exceptions or limitations to the reproduction right provided for in Article 2 in the following cases:
(b) in respect of reproductions on any medium made by a natural person for private use and for ends that are neither directly nor indirectly commercial, on condition that the rightholders receive fair compensation which takes account of the application or non-application of technological measures referred to in Article 6 to the work or subject-matter concerned."
Art. 5(5): "The exceptions and limitations provided for in paragraphs 1, 2, 3 and 4 shall only be applied in certain special cases which do not conflict with a normal exploitation of the work or other subject-matter and do not unreasonably prejudice the legitimate interests of the rightholder".

[159] Berne Convention for the Protection of Literary and Artistic Works of 9 September 1886, Art. 9(2): "It shall be a matter for legislation in the countries of the Union to permit the reproduction of such works in certain special cases, provided that such reproduction does not conflict with a normal exploitation of the work and does not unreasonably prejudice the legitimate interests of the author".

commercial distribution and benefit of their works. Secondly, big movie and music companies which act as copyright owners and ISPs simultaneously, such as *AOL Time Warner* in the United States, could gain an unfair advantage by reducing the level of levy offered to its clients. Thirdly, even simple browsing on Internet involves downloading of data associated with music or movies files and thus the private copyright levy would cover a vast amount of Internet users who do not use P2P networks at all.

However, some of the drawbacks might be overcome, if the levy system could be improved and sophisticated through the introduction of downloading thresholds or download quotas. For example, such national download limit could be imposed by a statutory licence and the levy would be payable if the particular Internet users exceed the download quota in question. Accordingly, subscribers who do not use P2P networks would not be affected. Subsequently, ISPs would charge users monthly according to the amount by which they had exceeded the downloading threshold and the accumulated sum would be passed to collecting society afterwards.[160] Therefore, the application of private copyright levy would constitute an effective scheme that could be implemented relatively easy and could resolve the issue of copyright infringement not only in respect of P2P networks, but in respect of all material from all Internet sources.

---

[160] C. Nasir, "Taming the beast of file-sharing - legal and technological solutions to the problem of copyright infringement over the Internet: Part 3" [2005] Ent. L.R. 16(5), 105-110.

6. CONCLUSION

It can be seen that the European national courts have relied on the long-standing civil doctrines of third party liability in cases related to illegal file sharing. By applying common set of civil rules, such as due care, knowledge or presumed knowledge and financial benefit, in general, courts have established P2P network providers' secondary liability successfully. Accordingly, as more of these elements are proved in a particular case, it is more likely an indirect infringement to be found. Hence, it can be said that traditional civil doctrines adopted by copyright law are still relevant in relation to the digital environment and new technologies, such as P2P software. Most of the decisions discussed above clearly indicate that protection of copyright holders' right is obligation for those P2P distributors who enable infringement for their own benefit. On the other hand, if a primary infringer has enjoyed a private use defence then it is more likely a secondary liability to be dismissed. Therefore, it can be concluded that the broad interpretation of private copyright exception in some European national jurisdictions creates certain issues in the application of secondary liability, but overall the copyright law in Europe have illustrated that it can appropriately deal with those problems spawned by new digital technologies.

Interpretation of the role of ISPs under the EU E-Commerce Directive from national courts definitely has favoured copyright holders in their attempts to tackle illegal file sharing. It can be noted that courts placed on ISPs liability that was broader than the intention of the Directive and more similar to that of the P2P service providers. As a result, the safe harbours immunities have been eroded and ISPs have been exposed significantly to a liability for copyright acts performed on their networks. However, European Court of Justice in *Productores de Musica de Espana Promusicae v. Telefonica de Espana*, by stating the conditions in which service providers may be compelled to disclose the personal data of their users, provided certain defence to ISPs.

It can be said that the vital role of ISPs as gatekeepers of Internet, which they must play in preventing copyright infringements, has not been clarified yet. It is clear that the development of P2P networks technology enabled users to benefit from cheap and unrestricted access of information contained published works. It also brought disturbance to copyright holders, namely that they would not be able to establish and control the digital market for their works. The private copyright levy solution, despite its drawbacks, provides unique business model which has not been available so far, namely to accept file sharing in exchange for indirect compensation. It is worth mentioning that in 2005 the French Parliament was discussing whether to impose such levy amounted to EUR 5 per month and to allow the P2P file sharing.[161]

---

[161] The idea was abandoned and replaced by a three strike law. According to it, new independent copyright enforcement authority (*HADOPI*) will first issue a warning to end subscriber who has exchanged unauthorised copyright material via P2P networks. In case of repeat, *HADOPI* may purpose from one to three months Internet access suspension to the user as settlement measure. If subscriber refuses proposed settlement and commits new infringement within one year of the first warning letter, then *HADOPI* may order the suspension of Internet access for a period of three months until one year. The proposed draft of three strike law was rejected from both French Constitutional Council (Court) (10 June 2009, see *note* 2) and European Parliament (European Parliament resolution of 10 April 2008 on cultural industries in Europe 2007/2153(INI), para. 23:"…

A levy system covering non-commercial file sharing provides an opportunity for copyright holders to avail themselves of the P2P technology where they would generate revenue from the massive use of their works. By securing compensation for right holders without hindering P2P networks, the private copyright levy would prevent the digital lock up of the on-line environment. The goal of copyright law, after all, is not to hamper new ways and technologies of exploitations, but to move and fit them within the limits of exclusive rights so that copyright holders to take advantage of such innovations for the benefit of both themselves and their clients – the Internet users.

---

calls on the Commission and the Member States, to avoid adopting measures conflicting with civil liberties and human rights and with the principles of proportionality, effectiveness and dissuasiveness, such as the interruption of Internet access").

- THE END -

7. BIBLIOGRAPHY

7.1 Books, Articles and Documents

E. Batalla, "Spain: Decision on file sharing for private use", Batalla Abodagos, Madrid, July 2006

T. O'Flynn, "File sharing: a holistic approach to the problem" Ent. L.R. [2006] 17(7), 218-221

M. Gillen, "File-sharing and individual civil liability in the United
Kingdom: a question of substantial abuse?" Ent. L.R. [2006] 17(1), 7-14

K. Koelman & B. Hugenholtz, "Online service provider liability for copyright liability" WIPO Workshop (9-10 December 1999)

H. Hartwig, "Online auctioneers must work harder in Germany", Bardehle Pagenberg Publications (2004)

GEMA Press Release January 2007, January 2008 and June 2009 (www.gema.de/en/press/press-releases)

R. W. Smith, "GEMA obtains injunctions against data exchange services", Berlin January 2007

J. Cheng, "No safe harbour for RapidShare in copyright infringement case", USA January 2008

N. Anderson, "Achtung! RapidShare ordered to filter all user uploads", USA, June 2009

Mikko Manner, "A Bittorrent P2P Network Shut Down and Its Operation Deemed Illegal in Finland" [2009] Ent.L.R. 20(1), 21–24

M. Manner, T. Siniketo & U. Polland, "The Pirate Bay Ruling – When the fun and games end" [2009] Ent. L.R. 201

K. Fiveash, "Mininova flattened by Dutch court", EPM Newsletter, the Netherlands, August 2009

M. Daly, "Life after Grokster: analysis of US and European approaches to file sharing" [2007] EIPR, 29(8), 319-324

O. Swartz, "Denmark and The Pirate Bay: Take it to the European Court of Justice", Sweden, February 2008

IFPI Digital Music Report, January 2008 (http://www.ifpi.org/content/library/dmr2008.pdf)

IFPI Chez Republic Press Release August 2009 (http://www.ifpicr.cz/?rubrika=1197)

IFPI Pres Release 4 April 2006 (http://www.ifpi.org/site-content/press/20060404a.html).

IFPI Digital Music Report, January 2009
(http://www.ifpi.org/content/section_resources/dmr2009.html)

P. Akester, "Copyright and the P2P challenge" [2005] EIPR, 27(3), 106-112

L. Huisman & G. J. V. Bergh, "Netherlands: copyright - file sharing service" [2002] Ent. L.R. 13(6), N77-78

J. Krikke, "Netherlands: copyright - infringement - file sharing and peer to peer technology" [2004] EIPR 26(4), N49

Pinto Ruiz & Del Valle Lawyers & Economists, Newsletter August 2009

S. W. Workman,"Developments in ISP Liability in Europe" Internet Law, August 2008

J. Dieselhorst "Germany: electronic commerce - liability of Internet Service Providers (ISPs)" [2000] CTLR 6(5), N67

R. Massey, "Independent service providers or industry's secret police? The role of the ISPs in relation to users infringing copyright" [2008] Ent. L.R. 19(7), 160-162

International Intellectual Property Alliance (IIPA) Special 301 Report on Copyright Protection and Enforcement, Spain 2009

A. Arena, "Monitoring the Activities of P2P Users Runs Foul of Privacy Legislation" IRIS Legal Observations of the European Audiovisual Observatory, July 2008

L. Hetherington, "Peer-to-peer file sharing - ISPs and disclosure of user identities" [2008] Ent. L.R. 19(4), 81-82

E. Prosperetti, "The Peppermint "Jam": peer-to-peer goes to court in Italy" [2008] Ent. L.R. 18(8), 280-283

C. Nasir, "Taming the beast of file-sharing - legal and technological solutions to the problem of copyright infringement over the Internet: Part 1" [2005] Ent. L.R. 16(3), 50-55

C. Nasir, "Taming the beast of file-sharing - legal and technological solutions to the problem of copyright infringement over the Internet: Part 1" [2005] Ent. L.R. 16(4), 82-88

C. Nasir, "From scare tactics to surcharges and other ideas: potential solutions to peer to peer copyright infringement: Part 3" [2005] Ent. L.R. 16(5), 105-110

C. Bernault & A. Lebois, "A Feasibility Study regarding a system of compensation for the exchange of works via the Internet" University of Nantes, June 2005 (http://alliance.bugiweb.com/usr/Documents/RapportUniversiteNantes-juin2005.pdf), edited by V. Grassmuck, Creative Commons Attribution – Share-Alike License © 2006

M. Williams & S. Seet, "Australia: copyright - infringement by operating file sharing on the internet" [2005] EIPR 27(12), N243

T. O'Shea, "BERR Consultation on legislative options to address illicit P2P file sharing" [2009] Ent. L.R. 20(1), 30-33

S. Yavorsky, "Copyright - music - piracy and file-sharing" [2006] Ent. L.R. 17(3), N23-25

C. Cifuentes & A. Fitzgerald, "Copyright and implied licences in shareware on the Internet" [1997] CTLR 3(5), 253-259

P. Akester & F. Lima, "Copyright and P2P: law, economics and patterns of evolution" [2006] EIPR 28(11), 576-579

F. von Lohmann, "Peer-to-Peer File Sharing and Copyright Law: A Primer for Developers" P2P and Copyright Law Presented at IPTPS '03 (February 2003)

M. Nwogugu, "The economics of digital content and illegal online file sharing: some legal issues" [2006] CTLR 2006 12(1), 5-13

S. Blakeney, "Peer-to-peer file sharing under assault" [2006] CTLR 12(2), 55-57

M. Scuffi, "The Enforcement of Intellectual Property Rights in Europe: Administration and Judiciary" Judge, World Intellectual Property Organization, March 2004 (WIPO/IPR/MCT/04/4)

J. Klosek & T. Gubins, "Competing Interests: Combating piracy and protecting privacy" published by BNA International, December 2008

A. Roosendaal, "Elimination of Anonymity in regard to Liability for Unlawful Acts on the Internet" Tilburg University, the Netherlands 2005 (http://arno.uvt.nl/show.cgi?fid=94167)

A. van Beelen, "The name behind the number" DLA Piper Publications, Amsterdam, December 2005

C. H. Massa & A. Strowel, "The scope of the proposed IP Enforcement Directive: torn between the desire to harmonise remedies and the need to combat piracy" [2004] EIPR 26(6), 244-253

H. K. Larusson, "Uncertainty in the scope of copyright: the case of illegal file-sharing in the UK" [2009] EIPR 31(3), 124-134

O. B. Vincents, "When rights clash online: the tracking of P2P copyright infringements vs. the EC Personal Data Directive" [2008] IJL & IT 16(3), 270-296

N. Jondet, "French Supreme Court allows tracking of P2P users" French Law in English, June 2007 (http://french-law.net/french-supreme-court-allows-tracking-of-p2p-users-ce-23-mai-2007.html)

R. W. Smith, "Public prosecutors refuse to collect IP address-related information from providers" Heise On-line Magazine, Berlin August 2007 (http://www.heise.de/english/newsticker/news/93759)

L. Sobel, "DRM as an Enabler of Business Models: ISPs as Digital Retailers" Berkeley Technology Law Journal 2003 (http://law.berkeley.edu/institutes/bclt/drm/papers/sobel-drm-btlj2003.html)

E. Batalla, "Spain: Decision on file sharing for private use" Batalla Abodagos, Madrid, July 2006

M. Starmer, "Video game company hunts down individual gamers in clampdown on illicit peer to peer file sharing" [2009] Ent. L.R. 20(1), 28-29

N. W. Netanel, "Impose a Non-commercial Use Levy to Allow Free Peer-to-Peer File-Sharing" [2003] 17 Harvard Journal of Law and Technology 1, 19-22

P. Wittgenstein, *Die digitale Agenda der WIPO-Vertrage*, Bern Switzerland: Stampfli (2000)

A. A. Wandtke, "Copyright und virtueller Markt in der Informationsgesellschaft" GRUG 49 (1), 7 (2002)

C. Geiger, "Right to Copy v. Three-Step Test, „The Future of the Private Copy Exception in the Digital Environment" (2005) Computer Law Review International (1), 7

A. N. Dixon, "Liability of users and third parties for copyright infringements on the internet: overview of international developments" (*Peer-to-peer file sharing and secondary liability in copyright law* edited by A. Strowel, Edward Elgar 2009)

J. C. Ginsburg, "Copyright control v. compensation: the prospects for exclusive rights after *Grokster* and *Kazaa*" (*Peer-to-peer file sharing and secondary liability in copyright law* edited by A. Strowel, Edward Elgar 2009)

G. W. Austin, "Global networks and domestic laws: some private international law issues arising from Australian and US liability theories" (*Peer-to-peer file sharing and secondary liability in copyright law* edited by A. Strowel, Edward Elgar 2009)

A. Peukert, "A bipolar copyright system for the digital network environment" (*Peer-to-peer file sharing and secondary liability in copyright law* edited by A. Strowel, Edward Elgar 2009)

R. Clark, "Sharing out online liability: sharing files, sharing risks and targeting ISPs" (*Peer-to-peer file sharing and secondary liability in copyright law* edited by A. Strowel, Edward Elgar 2009)

J. H. Reichman, G. B. Dinwoodie & P. Samielson, "A reverse notice and takedown regime to enable public interest uses of technically protected copyright works" (*Peer-to-peer file sharing and secondary liability in copyright law* edited by A. Strowel, Edward Elgar 2009)

L. Lessig, *The Future of Ideas*, Random House, New York (2001)

L. Guibault, *Copyright Limitations and Contracts: An Analysis of the Contractual Overridability of Limitations on Copyright*, Kluwer Law International (2002)

G. J.H. Smith, *International Law and Regulations*, Sweet & Maxwell 4th edition (2007)

W.R. Cornish & D. Llewlelyn, *Cornish & Llewlelyn Intellectual Property, Patents, Copyrights, Trademarks and Allied Rights*, Sweet & Maxwell 6th edition (2007)

P. Torremans, *Holyoak & Torremans Intellectual Property Law*, OUP 5th edition (2008)

J.A.L Sterling, *World Copyright Law*, Sweet & Maxwell 3rd edition (2008)

P. Akester, A practical guide to digital copyright law, Sweet & Maxwell (2008)

7.2 Cases

Monrex Rolex v. Ricardo No I ZR 304/01 German Civil Supreme Court, 2004

Polydor v. Brown [2005] EWHC 3191

Société Civile des Producteurs Phonographiques v. Anthony G 31 chambre/2 (8 December 2005).

Gershwin Publishing v. Columbia Artist Management 1162 (2d Cir. 1971)

Sony Corp. v. Universal City Studios 464 US 417 (1984)

Shapiro, Bernstein & Co v. H.L. Green 306 (2d Cir. 1963)

A & M v. Napster 114 F. Supp.2d 896 (N.D. Call. 2000)

MGM Studio v. Grokster 125 S. Ct. 2764 (2005)

Falcon v. Famous Players Film [1926] 2 KB 474

Adelaide Corp. v. Australasian Performing Right Association [1928] 40 CLR 481

University of New South Wales v. Moorhouse [1975] 133 CLR 1

Universal Music Australia v. Sharman Licence Holding [2005] FCA 1242

Sony Music v. Easyinternetcafe [2003] EWHC 62

CBS Records v. Amstrad [1988] AC 1013

In The Koursk [1924] All ER Rep 168

TONO v. Bruvik Case No 2004/822, Supreme Court, Norway (25 January 2005)

Kazaa v. Buma/Stemra No KG 01/2264 OdC, Amsterdam District Court (29 November 2001)

Kazaa v. Buma/Stemra No 1370/01 SKG, Court of Appeals, Netherlands (28 March 2002)

Stichting BREIN v. KPN No 276747, Hague Court, Netherlands (5 January 2007)

Stichting BREIN v. Leaseweb BV No 369220/KG ZA 07-850, Amsterdam District Court (27.06.2007)

The Pirate Bay Docket no. B 13301-06, Stockholm District Court, Sweden (17 April 2009).

SAGE v. Elrincondejesus, Mercantile Court No 7, Barcelona, Judge Raul N. Garcia (2 July 2007).

Hi Bit Software v. AOL Bertelsmann Online [2002] ECDR 27 (8 March 2001)

Perathoner v. S. Joseph Societe Free [2003] ECDR 8 (23 May 2001)

Church of Spiritual Technology v. Dataweb BV [2004] ECDR 25 (4 September 2003)

IFPI v. TDC Case No U2006.1474H, Danish Supreme Court (10 February 2006)

*IFPI Danmark v. Tele2*Case No FI15124/2006, Copenhagen City Court (25 October 2006)

IFPI v. DMT2/Tele2 No FS 14324/2007 (5 February 2008)

SABAM v. SA Scarlet Cardozo Arts & Entertainment Journal Translation Series #001, Case No 04/8975, Brussels District Court (29 June 2007)

BREIN v. UPC (Chello) No 194741/KGZA-05-462/BL/EV, Utrecht District Court (12 July 2005)

Norwich Pharmacal v. Customs and Excise Commissioners [1974] AC 133

EMI Records v. Eircom[2006] ECDR 5

Productores de Musica de Espana Promusicae v. Telefonica de Espana Case C-275/06 [2008] ECDR

Case No 28 O 634/05 Koln District Court, 2005

Case No 308 O 41/06 Hamburg District Court, 2006

Topware Interactive v. Barwinska Decision of Patents County Court, August 2009

Stichting BREIN v. Mininova EPM Newsletter, the Netherlands, August 2009

Lycos v. Pessers Danish Supreme Court (25 November 2005)

GEMA v. RapidShare GEMA Press Release January 2007, January 2008 and June 2009 (www.gema.de/en/press/press-releases)

www.ingramcontent.com/pod-product-compliance
Lightning Source LLC
Chambersburg PA
CBHW070917180526
45168CB00005B/2045